smart kids,
better grades

How to Make Your Child
A BETTER LISTENER

by Florence Karnofsky and Trudy Weiss

Fearon Teacher Aids
A Division of Frank Schaffer Publica

D1416677

This Fearon Teacher Aids product was formerly manufactured and distributed by American Teaching Aids, Inc., a subsidiary of Silver Burdett Ginn, and is now manufactured and distributed by Frank Schaffer Publications, Inc. FEARON, FEARON TEACHER AIDS, and the FEARON balloon logo are marks used under license from Simon & Schuster, Inc.

Editorial Director: Virginia L. Murphy
Editor: Virginia Massey Bell
Copyeditor: Kristin Eclov
Cover Design: Lucyna Green
Design: Teena Remer

Fearon Teacher Aids
A Division of Frank Schaffer Publication, Inc.
23740 Hawthorne Boulevard
Torrance, CA 90505-5927

IISBN 0-86653-933-6

Printed in the United States of America

1.9 8 7 6

Acknowledgments

Illustrations in this book were drawn by the children at Nathan Hale Elementary School in Lansing, Illinois, and George Bibich Elementary in Dyer, Indiana. A special thanks to Laura Judkis for her drawings on pages 1, 27, 50, and 51 and to Ben Weiss for his drawing on page 17.

We'd like to acknowledge the following for their suggestions:

Dennis Soustek, Principal
Heritage Middle School
Lansing, IL

Marie M. Meyer, Ed. D., Director
Thornton Fractional Area Educational Cooperative
Calumet City, IL

Karen R. Scott, Reading Specialist
District #155
Calumet City, IL

Dedication

This book is dedicated to the many children
who taught us so much over the years.

About the Authors

Trudy Weiss spent eighteen years teaching
in grades one through eight, two years
as a teacher of learning disabled children,
and three years as a curriculum coordinator.
She has also coauthored several articles
for several teacher magazines.

Florence Karnofsky has taught elementary children
in Indiana and Pennsylvania for twenty-five years,
specializing in the areas of science and social studies.

CONTENTS

INTRODUCTION

● ● ● ● ● ● ● ● ● ● ● ● ● ● ● ● ●

HOW THIS BOOK CAN HELP YOU

Listening is a skill—and like any skill, it can be taught. For many years, teachers and parents have assumed that listening ability develops in children as naturally as vision. Today, we know better. There is more to listening than being able to hear. Listening includes learning how to concentrate, understanding what is being said, and responding appropriately to directions— with each part directly related to how a child learns in school.

Teachers have always known that children cannot be successful in school unless they are good listeners. In the elementary grades, children spend approximately 60% of their time listening to the teacher. They listen to explanations, directions, and questions. In high school and college, students spend over 90% of the classroom time listening.

Children who know how to listen have an easier time paying attention in class, understanding the information that is taught, and correctly following directions. Many schools are now teaching listening strategies. Some teachers give listening drills; others teach listening in conjunction with subjects. Today, children are tested for their listening ability by nationally standardized tests. As parents, it is important for you to understand the rewards for helping your child improve his or her listening skills.

Children who do not know how to listen in school often do not listen to their parents at home either. For parents and teachers, it's a frustrating problem. When Mother says "Camille, it's time for you to go to bed," Camille doesn't listen. When the teacher says "Listen carefully, because there are several steps to the assignment," Camille continues to rearrange items in her pencil box. When her report card comes home marked "Doesn't listen," Mother or Dad scold Camille, but scolding alone doesn't help. Nothing will help until Camille is taught how to listen at home and at school.

Parents do not have to be convinced that life would be easier if their children listened. *How to Make Your Child a Better Listener* explains what you, as parents, can do to develop your child's listening ability.

By following our simple suggestions, your reward will be a child who listens at home and has the potential for earning better grades at school.

CHAPTER 1

MY CHILD DOESN'T LISTEN TO ME

"I thought I was listening, but the teacher said I wasn't."

LISTENING IS MORE THAN HEARING

When a teacher says "Mario is a good listener," he or she means:

1. He pays attention (concentration).

2. He comprehends what was said (understanding).

3. He reacts appropriately to what he heard (response).

When a mother says "Jimmy doesn't listen," she probably means Jimmy doesn't do as he is told. Responding appropriately is only one aspect of listening. In this book, when we use the word "listening," it will include three components:

Concentration—paying attention to what is said

Understanding—comprehending what is said

Response—responding appropriately to what is said

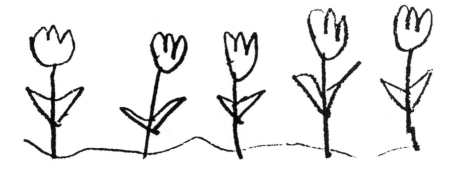

8

CONCENTRATION MEANS PAYING ATTENTION TO WHAT IS SAID: THE STORY OF CAMILLE

Camille at School

Camille is ten years old and in the fifth grade. She is about one year behind in reading and math, and every night Camille has to call her friend to get her homework assignment. Her work is often incorrectly or incompletely done.

Camille at Home

Mother: Camille, would you bring me the clothes in the laundry basket?

Camille: (Goes to her room and returns a minute later.) What did you want?

What is causing Camille's problem? It seems clear enough that Camille is not paying attention when her mother or her teacher speaks. She lacks the skill of concentrating on what is being said.

Reasons why children do not pay attention are explained (with tips on how to develop attention skills) in Chapter 2.

UNDERSTANDING WHAT IS SAID IS LISTENING COMPREHENSION: THE STORY OF ABBY

Abby at School

Abby is seven. She is a quiet child. In class, she rarely speaks a word. She pays attention, but she doesn't understand what the teacher is saying. The teacher's words confuse her and she doesn't know how to tell her teacher that she doesn't understand. Abby tries very hard to pay attention, but is having a lot of difficulty learning because she lacks listening comprehension.

Abby at Home

Mom: Abby, didn't I ask you to tell Dad to pick up my dress at the cleaners?

Abby: I didn't hear you.

Abby is a little girl who wants to do what she is supposed to. She also wants to do well in school. Her problem is that she has a difficult time understanding spoken language. Abby lacks listening comprehension skills.

Why children lack listening comprehension and how this skill can easily be developed is explained in Chapter 4.

RESPONSE MEANS REACTING APPROPRIATELY TO WHAT IS SAID: THE STORY OF SHAWN AND MARIO

Shawn is four. At the end of the day, Mrs. Dodd says "Children, place your drawings on the table, pick up all the crayons and put them in the bucket, and then get into line." Shawn ignores Mrs. Dodd's instructions about the drawings and crayons and rushes to be first in line.

Mario is also four. Mario listens to Mrs. Dodd and places his drawing on the table, helps pick up the crayons, and then lines up with the rest of the children. Mario is the kind of child who makes life easy for parents and teachers.

He pays attention, he understands what is said to him, and then he responds appropriately.

Why both boys have such different listening habits and how Shawn's habits can be improved is explained in Chapter 5.

By dividing listening into the three components— concentration, understanding, and response— we believe it will help parents better understand what listening really is and how to help their child improve his or her listening habits at home and at school.

We shall discuss each component of listening separately, although it is important to know that all components are interrelated. Each component is dependent upon the other. It is not possible to understand something without paying attention to what is being said. Similarly, it is not possible to respond appropriately without comprehending.

HOW TO JUDGE YOUR CHILD'S LISTENING ABILITY

Together, concentration, understanding, and response are important factors in your child's listening ability. If you find yourself saying "Richard never listens to me," or your daughter's report card comes home from school with the written message "Rachel doesn't pay attention," ask yourself the following questions:

1. Does my child pay attention when I talk to him or her?

2. Does he or she understand what I am saying?

3. Does my child respond appropriately to my requests?

Answering each question separately will help you determine if your child has a listening problem. On the following page is an informal quiz which may help you evaluate your child's listening ability. Once you understand the three components of listening, there are many ways you can help improve your child's listening skill.

1. **Listening Is a Habit That Can Be Taught at Home and at School.**

2. **Poor Listeners Can Become Good Listeners.**

3. **Good Listeners Can Become Even Better Listeners.**

HOW GOOD IS YOUR CHILD'S LISTENING ABILITY?

Following is a list of questions about typical home experiences. The questions will help you evaluate your child's ability to concentrate, understand, and respond appropriately. Some of the questions listed below may not be appropriate for all age levels. If this is the case, think of appropriate situations in which your child would need to listen to directions. Then ask yourself questions pertaining to those situations. Answer "yes" or "no" to each question.

		YES	NO
1.	Do I have to tell my child more than once when I want him or her to do something?	❏	❏
2.	Does my child daydream when I talk to him or her?	❏	❏
3.	Does he or she say "I didn't hear you?"	❏	❏
4.	Is he or she impatient when I try to explain something to him or her?	❏	❏
5.	Does my child forget what he or she did in preschool or school?	❏	❏
6.	Does he or she forget to give me written messages from school?	❏	❏
7.	Is my child inattentive when I try to read to him or her?	❏	❏
8.	Does my child have difficulty following directions with two or three steps, such as	❏	❏

(1) In the bathroom cupboard are two bars of soap.

(2) Would you bring one to me?

(3) Put the other one in the downstairs bathroom.

9.	Does my child have trouble telling me about the television program he or she just watched?	❏	❏
10.	When I give my child a message for another person, does he or she forget what the message was?	❏	❏

"No" answers indicate good listening ability.

7 to 10   good

3 to 6   average

0 to 2   needs improvement

SCHOOLS GIVE LISTENING TESTS

Listening ability is extremely important to increasing a child's vocabulary and understanding of the subject matter taught in school. In fact, listening ability is so important that it is included in school achievement tests.

TYPES OF LISTENING QUESTIONS FOUND IN FIRST, THIRD, AND SIXTH-GRADE SCHOOL ACHIEVEMENT TESTS

School listening tests usually have two parts. The first section tests a child's listening vocabulary. The child marks the appropriate answer on an answer sheet.

An example of a first-grade listening vocabulary question is:

The rear of the room is in the…
front…
side…
back.

As the children progress through the grades, the words get more difficult.

An example of a third-grade listening vocabulary question is:

To perform is to…
follow…
act…
eat.

An example of a sixth-grade listening vocabulary question is:

Something which is medieval is from…
Colonial times…
Greek times…
one hundred years ago…
before modern times.

The second listening part of an achievement test involves listening comprehension. Teachers read paragraphs aloud and then ask the students questions about each example. The children mark the appropriate answers on a special answer sheet. Since the paragraphs test the child's listening ability, each paragraph is read only once.

The teacher reads the following paragraph aloud:

Amy, Billy, and Janet went with mother on a picnic. They played on the swings and had lunch at a picnic table. The children had a good time and enjoyed the activities.

Mark an "X" under the picture which shows where the children ate lunch. (It is important for younger children to use visual clues to answer the questions. The choices include a picture of a restaurant, a kitchen, and a park.)

An example of a third-grade listening comprehension question is:

The teacher reads the following paragraph aloud:

Methods of communication have changed over the years. Native Americans sent smoke signals to tribes far away. During the time of George Washington, people could send letters by horseback or boat. It took many weeks and even months to hear from friends who lived far away. Now friends can be reached by telephone in a few minutes, no matter how far away they live.

The main idea of this story is: friends...
far away places...
sending messages.
(The children mark the appropriate answer on the answer sheet.)

An example of a sixth-grade listening comprehension question is:

The teacher reads the following paragraph aloud:

The five members of the Gallegos family were on a spring vacation. They spent one week in Chicago visiting many museums. Sammy, age seven, loved the Natural History Museum. Mary Anne, age three, wanted to spend all her time at the Children's Expressway Museum. The Planetarium excited Betsy, who was in junior high school. Dad liked the Museum of Science and Industry the best, while Mom loved the Art Institute.

How many places did the family visit?
two...
three...
four...
five?

At the end of the vacation the family was probably:
surprised...
frightened...
unaware...
tired.

The month the family went on vacation was probably:
December...
June...
April...
September.

(The children mark the appropriate answers on the answer sheet.)

CHAPTER 2
● ● ● ● ● ● ● ● ● ● ● ● ● ● ● ● ● ●
CONCENTRATION: DOES YOUR CHILD PAY ATTENTION WHEN YOU TALK?

Learning to pay attention is the first step in learning to listen. Following are typical examples of occasions when children must pay attention in order to be successful in school.

CONCENTRATION IS PAYING ATTENTION TO WHAT IS BEING SAID: PAYING ATTENTION AT SCHOOL

Travis is six years old and it is his first day at school. He is wearing new jeans and a striped shirt. He's eager, but also anxious. Will Mrs. Dodd, his teacher, be mean? What if he has to go to the bathroom? What if he doesn't get on the right bus when it's time to go home? Will the other children be nice to him?

Mrs. Dodd greets the children at the classroom door with a smile and friendly words. She then begins to give directions. It is important for the children to listen carefully. At various times during the first few days, Mrs. Dodd will explain to the children:

1. Where to sit

2. Where to hang their sweaters

3. Where to place their book bags

4. Where the bathroom is

5. What to do if they must use the bathroom

6. How to buy their lunches or what to do if they brought their lunches from home

7. What to do if they feel sick

8. Where the nurse's office is

9. Which door to use when entering the school building

10. Which bus to take

11. The rules for recess

And that is only the beginning. The children must also listen to directions about books, paper, pencils, crayons, and the learning activities that Mrs. Dodd has planned for the day.

Travis must absorb all this information by paying attention to what Mrs. Dodd says. If Travis is able to understand all the directions, he will be taking the first step to being successful in school. He will know what to do—and he will feel good about school and himself.

WHY CHILDREN MUST CONCENTRATE IN MR. HEIDEN'S CLASS

The children in Mr. Heiden's fifth-grade class are about ten years old. When he assigns a research report, the children will have to pay attention to directions considerably more advanced than Mrs. Dodd's. For example:

1. Choose a subject for your report.

2. Make a list of topics you think should be investigated.

3. Use at least three references, not counting the encyclopedia.

4. Make sure the references you have chosen are not too difficult or too easy.

5. Take notes on 3" x 5" (7.6 cm x 12.7 cm) cards.

6. Put the topic title at the top of each card.

7. Notes need not be in complete sentences.

8. Complete your note-taking by Friday.

9. Use homework time to work on your report, if necessary.

WHY SOME CHILDREN DON'T CONCENTRATE

Many children enter school ready to concentrate. They know what "paying attention" means and they are eager to do so. Often these children have attended preschools where they acquired this habit.

Other children are not able to concentrate in school because they:

1. Feel sleepy or tired

2. Feel fidgety

3. Are not accustomed to paying attention when parents speak

4. Are busy daydreaming

5. Play with objects in their desks

6. Do not see the value of learning

7. Are easily distracted and only half pay attention

THE CHILD WHO PAYS ATTENTION AT HOME KNOWS HOW TO CONCENTRATE AT SCHOOL

If children have been taught to pay attention at home, they will most likely do the same at school. They won't be perfect every day. Some days they'll do better than others, but on most days they will be able to concentrate.

19

HOW CHILDREN LEARN TO CONCENTRATE AT HOME

Mother: Jason, say "Mommy.... Mommy...."

Jason: Mmmmmmmmmmm mmmmmmmmmma

Dad: My turn now. Jason, say "Daddeee."

INFANTS LEARN QUICKLY TO PAY ATTENTION

It is startling to realize how quickly after birth infants begin paying attention. Within a month or so, as Jason's eyes, ears, and brain develop, he responds to his mother's cooing and singing with a smile. Then his eyes follow her, paying attention to her movements. He concentrates on the brightly colored rattle his father shakes and before long he is reaching out to grab it. Through paying attention, Jason is learning.

Throughout those first months of his life, as his parents lovingly and encouragingly talked to him, Jason paid attention to the shaping of their mouths and listened to the sounds coming from their throats. He concentrated on them—and finally he was able to imitate them. By the time he was a little over one year old, Jason could talk—a remarkable achievement resulting from paying attention and hearing.

Paying attention is a natural process stimulated by parents talking and playing with their children. As children grow older, they are able to pay attention for longer and longer periods of time. The average three-year-old has an attention span of approximately five minutes, a six-year-old, twenty minutes, and a ten-year-old, thirty minutes.

WHAT PARENTS CAN DO TO ENCOURAGE CONCENTRATION

Parents cannot push their children to concentrate beyond their natural capacity, but they can encourage optimum growth in these ways:

1. Talk about a variety of subjects with your child. By participating in conversations with you, your child learns to pay attention to your words.

2. Read and tell interesting stories that hold your child's attention. If appropriate, encourage your child to tell you simple stories as well.

3. Play games with your child that require following instructions and paying attention to one another's words, such as "Simon Says" or "Captain May I?"

4. Play records or cassettes that tell stories.

5. Sing to your child, emphasizing the words.

Occasionally, a parent might notice that a child has limited responses to sound and spoken words. These children may have physical hearing problems that should be checked. Today, many preschools and most grade schools routinely test children's hearing.

SOME SYMPTOMS OF POSSIBLE HEARING PROBLEMS

1. Has poor pronunciation
2. Speaks too loudly or too softly
3. Cups ear when trying to hear
4. Leans forward or stands too close
5. Turns head to one side
6. Appears not to understand
7. Gets upset for no apparent reason

Still other children are captives of their bodies. Some six to ten-year-olds can't sit still for more than a minute or two. They jump, tumble, and roll, oblivious to the sounds of voices around them. These children, too, may need medical attention.

It is not uncommon to find children falling asleep at school because they stay up late on week days to watch television. These children have trouble concentrating at school because they haven't had enough sleep.

Finally, there are children who tune other people out. They become absorbed in their personal play, in television, a book, friends, or daydreams. These children can be helped to learn to pay attention by following the simple techniques described below:

1. Maintain eye contact. Don't call out instructions from another room. Wait to give instructions or ask a question until you are looking directly into your child's eyes.

2. Touch your child. With your hand, gently raise your child's chin so that his or her eyes are looking into yours. Or, hold your child's hand or touch his or her shoulder in order to get his or her attention before you utter a single word.

3. Ask your child to repeat what you said. This encourages concentration and allows you to check to make sure your child heard the directions correctly.

4. Before giving directions or information, set the stage for listening.

   Example:
   Mother: Tim, please come into the kitchen right away. I want to talk to you.

5. Give your child your complete attention when talking. If you have something of importance to say to your child, stop whatever you are doing before you say it. If you are reading the newspaper, stop for a minute while you talk to your child. Get eye to eye contact before giving instructions. If you do not give your child your undivided attention when you talk to him or her, you will not receive undivided attention in return. By your own behavior, you are indicating the behavior you expect from your child, too.

6. When your child wants to talk to you, stop what you are doing and give your child your complete attention. You are setting an example for how important it is to listen and pay attention when someone else is talking. This is particularly important when preparing your child for school. Establishing good listening skills will help your child be better prepared for learning in school.

7. Try not to interrupt play activity if your child is in deep concentration. Concentration doesn't develop in a single session. It takes developmental readiness and repeated practice until paying attention becomes a habit.

Use the checklist on page 23 as a tool to evaluate your child's ability to concentrate. This is a good indicator of how well your child's listening skills are developing. Being able to pay attention is the first step to learning how to listen.

DOES YOUR CHILD CONCENTRATE?

Does your child:

		YES	NO
1.	Look you in the eye when you speak?	❑	❑
2.	Stand (or sit) still when spoken to?	❑	❑
3.	Appear interested in what you say?	❑	❑
4.	Stick to the subject when you speak?	❑	❑
5.	Usually remember what you said?	❑	❑
6.	Show patience when you explain something?	❑	❑
7.	Listen attentively to a story?	❑	❑
8.	Listen to records and cassettes?	❑	❑
9.	Retell a story?	❑	❑
10.	Repeat what you said when asked?	❑	❑
11.	Remain attentive, even with moderate noises in the room?	❑	❑

"Yes" answers to most of the questions indicate good listening ability.

7 to 11	good
3 to 6	average
0 to 2	needs improvement

23

CHAPTER 3

UNDERSTANDING: DOES YOUR CHILD COMPREHEND WHEN LISTENING?

"I listen faster than my teacher speaks."

Valerie

"My teacher tells me too much."

Scott

UNDERSTANDING MEANS COMPREHENDING WHAT IS BEING SAID

In every grade from kindergarten through college, poor comprehension can be a major problem. Without language comprehension, children cannot understand what they are hearing or reading. How well children understand what they are hearing contributes significantly to their success or failure in school.

As we indicated earlier, the three components of listening are all interrelated. It is obvious that children who do not pay attention will have trouble with comprehension. Yet many children who try very hard to pay attention also have trouble understanding what they are hearing.

Case History: Valerie

Valerie Hubbard is eight years old. She's in Ms. Vimco's third-grade classroom. To her teacher, Valerie is an intriguing puzzle. Although her scores on tests of mental abilities indicate she is within the range of average, from the day she entered school, Valerie earned top grades.

"What do you do at home," Ms. Vimco asked Valerie's mother, "that makes your daughter such an enthusiastic and diligent worker? She's interested in everything. She has ideas and she's not timid about expressing them. She has excellent listening comprehension and as soon as she knows what's expected of her, she's off like a whiz."

"Well, I can't really say," said Mrs. Hubbard. "Maybe it's because I talk to her so much. From the day Valerie was born, I began talking to her. She'd be lying in her crib and I'd be explaining to her how to do this or that. If I were washing, I'd tell her about detergents, water softeners, and spot removers. It sounds silly, doesn't it? I've always explained to her everything I do. My husband's a talker, too. Some people would call us gabbers. But that's

about what we do. We just talk to her."

Lucky Valerie! When she entered school, she had already had lots of practice concentrating on what her parents were saying. In addition, because she heard so much spoken language at home, it was easy for her to understand spoken language at school.

Elementary children spend over 60% of their time in the classroom listening. If they are not able to understand what is said, they will have a difficult time learning in school. Therefore, it is important to spend as much time as possible talking with your child. Talking will improve your child's ability to listen and understand the concepts taught in school.

WHAT MS. VIMCO EXPECTS FROM HER THIRD GRADERS

Much of what children learn in third grade, they learn through spoken language. In Ms. Vimco's class, the following are the types of directions and explanations the students need to be able to understand:

1. How to multiply with one and two-digit multipliers.

2. How to write in complete sentences.

3. How to divide a notebook into sections according to subjects.

4. The homework assignment for the night.

5. How to go to the gym for a program.

6. How to devise a costume for a play.

7. How to use watercolor paints.

8. How to play kickball.

9. When and how to divide double consonants into syllables.

10. How to find books in the school library for a topical report.

11. How to write cursive letters.

12. How to work well in a group.

In Ms. Vimco's class, not every child is like Valerie. Even though Ms. Vimco uses language appropriate for the grade level, some children have difficulty understanding her words. They may have trouble comprehending directions, the words Ms. Vimco uses may be unfamiliar, or they may have trouble forming mental images from what she says. The following are typical examples of what occurs when children have trouble understanding spoken language:

After reading and discussing with the children a story about Abraham Lincoln,

Ms. Vimco asks the children to write a story beginning with "If I were Mr. Lincoln, I would…"

Josh is upset because he doesn't know what to write. He did not understand most of the story.

Later, Ms. Vimco tells the children that in order to memorize their spelling words they should first look at a word, say it out loud, and then close their eyes and try spelling it. The students should then check to see if they spelled the word correctly. Finally, they should write each spelling word three times.

Chris looks at the spelling words, closes her eyes, and then forgets what she is supposed to do. She has trouble remembering directions with more than one or two steps.

Finally, Ms. Vimco gives the children instructions for weaving Valentine placemats. She tells the students to glue the tip of each white strip along the top of the red paper.

Instead of the tip of the white strip, Jim glues the entire strip to the red paper. He misunderstood the directions.

WHY SOME CHILDREN HAVE PROBLEMS UNDERSTANDING

In every grade, there are children who, even though they pay attention, have difficulty understanding lessons. The reasons may vary:

1. Not all children are born with the same ability to learn. Some learn rapidly, others more slowly.

2. Some children are not good auditory learners. They learn better visually—by seeing examples and demonstrations rather than only by hearing.

3. Some children are overly anxious or nervous. They are unable to concentrate and, therefore, do not comprehend well.

4. Some children do not hear much spoken language at home, or their home language is different from that spoken at school.

5. Some children have not learned to concentrate. They have difficulty paying attention, which leads to problems in understanding what is being taught.

PARENTS AND TEACHERS CAN TEACH BETTER LISTENING HABITS

In Mr. Heiden's room there are 27 children, each different from the other. The progress they achieve in fifth grade depends on the teacher, the children, and their parents. How parents can help children develop good listening comprehension is explained in the following chapter.

CHAPTER 4
●●●●●●●●●●●●●●●●●●
HOW YOU CAN INCREASE YOUR CHILD'S LISTENING COMPREHENSION

The more language children hear and the more words they know, the greater their understanding will be. When children talk with parents, grandparents, brothers and sisters, neighbors, playmates, and friends, they are learning and getting practice in comprehending spoken language. An average child knows about 500 words by the age of two and 5,000 by the age of six, simply through hearing people talk.

The greater the variety of words parents use, the greater the number of words children will learn. The more ideas parents express verbally, the more their children will be stimulated to express ideas of their own. Parents who, like Valerie's mother, spend a great deal of time talking with their children are more likely to find their children doing well at school. Their children will be more likely to understand their teachers, be able to express their own thoughts, and adequately follow directions.

When talking to children, remember to use a variety of words. A child is introduced to a larger vocabulary just by listening to his or her parents talk. For example, you can sharpen your description of a man by using any number of these words:

handsome	tall
strong	muscular
athletic	humorous
bent	graceful
thin	slender
young	interesting
tired	happy
unhappy	dignified
well-dressed	elderly

One easy way to enlarge your child's vocabulary is to use specific words instead of general ones. For example:

General	Specific
I need to water the plants.	I need to water the African violets and the philodendron.
It's cold outside.	The temperature outside is 14°F (7.8°C)
I guess you won't have school tomorrow.	Tomorrow is Thanksgiving Day. Do you know what that means?

IF SOMEONE ELSE IS CARING FOR YOUR CHILD

Today, while both parents work, many children are being cared for by relatives, neighbors, and in a variety of preschools. At a time of their lives when children easily and rapidly learn language, parents should investigate how much oral communication their children will have with their caregivers during the day.

In a day-care situation, it is not enough that babies be fed and kept dry. They need to be talked to, not just at feeding time, but throughout the day. It is not sufficient for children to be allowed to sit in front of a television set all day or kept busy with crayons, blocks, and toy cars unless occasionally a caregiver is interacting with them, too.

The preschool years are too important to listening comprehension to allow them to be lived in silence.

Encourage your caregiver to interact with your children in small groups, reading stories, asking questions, and talking about the day's events. Or, as an ending to a day at the day care, plan to sit together with your child and talk about what he or she did that day, the books they read, or the games they played. Talking together, listening to stories, and recalling events of the day will help improve your child's listening ability.

WHAT SHALL WE TALK ABOUT?

Teaching children to understand language need not be difficult. It requires neither lots of time nor lots of money. All parents need to do is talk to their children while they are doing dishes, driving a car, washing clothes, watering the flowers, and so on. Hundreds of subjects in your own life will be interesting to talk about with your child. As you talk with your child, it is important to give your undivided attention to what he or she is saying. This behavior shows your child that what he or she has to say is important to you. You are also saying that you expect the same kind of undivided attention from your child as well. For example:

1. If you work outside the home, talk about all the things you do when you leave home.

Where do you work?

How do you get there?

What goods or services does your company produce or provide?

What is the name of your job?

What kind of equipment do you use?

What do you like or dislike about your job?

What training did you
need for your job?

Who are the people
you meet
every day?

2. Talk about your
house.

Where does the
water supply
come from?

How does the furnace
spread the heat
throughout the house?

Why do you water and
fertilize your lawn?

What materials were
needed to build your
house?

What would your ideal
house look like?

Whenever you are
making a repair to your
house, explain to your
child what you are
doing and why.

3. Talk about your family.

Who are your relatives
and how are they
related to one another?

Where do your relatives
live?

How does your family
spend money?

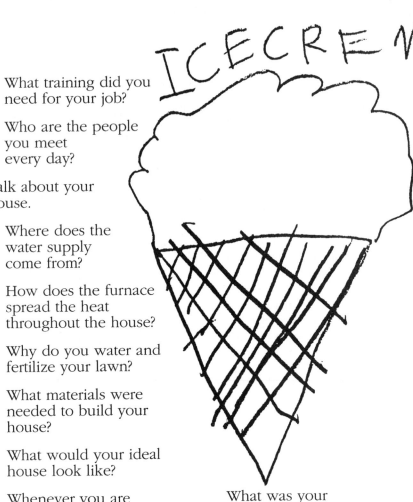

What was your
childhood like?

Where would you like
to go on a family
vacation?

4. Talk about climate and
the weather.

Explain what is meant
by degrees.

What is meant by
freezing, above zero,
and below zero?

Explain dry spell,
cold spell, heat spell.

When they occur,
explain frost, dew, hail,
sleet, humidity,
tornadoes, and
hurricanes.

Explain the difference
between a thermometer
and a thermostat.

If you visit other
sections of the country,
discuss differences in
climate and geography.

Talk about the weather
as described on
television.

5. Talk about holidays.

What are their names?
What do they mean?

Who or what do they
celebrate?

When and how did
they begin?

Does everybody in the
country celebrate the
same holidays?

Is it a national, local, or
religious holiday?

Do other countries
celebrate the same
holiday?

What special foods are
eaten on these
holidays? Why?

What customs are
followed on a particular
holiday by most
people?

What special customs do you follow?

6. Talk about time.

   Preschoolers can understand days, weeks, months, and years.

   Explain hours, minutes, seconds.

   Discuss the characteristics of the four seasons as they arrive in your area.

   Discuss the behavior of birds, animals, and changes in vegetation as the seasons come and go.

7. Talk about geography when you are riding in your car.

Are you riding through a city, town, village, or countryside?

How do mountains, hills, and plains differ?

Where does the river come from?

What is the difference between a river, a lake, an ocean or a creek?

What is an earthquake?

What is the difference between a street, a highway, an interstate, and a turnpike?

8. Talk about your shopping.

   What fabric are you looking for and why?

Why do you like or dislike a particular store?

What are sales and discounts?

How do credit cards and bank checks work?

Discuss in what countries your purchases were manufactured. Locate these countries on a map.

9. Ask questions that arouse curiosity.

What causes shadows?

Why do dandelions come up every year?

Why does a car need water and gasoline?

Where does butter come from?

Why do we need to put stamps on letters?

In addition to providing practice with paying attention and understanding, home conversations provide a background that helps children be active participants in school discussions. Prior knowledge helps children understand the content in their textbooks and also builds confidence and self-esteem.

TREATING CHILDREN'S TALK WITH RESPECT

When adults listen to children, they are teaching children to listen, too. When children express opinions or ask questions, they deserve the respect and courtesy that parents want when they speak as well. Children also deserve praise for being interested and thoughtful. For example, the following statements to children can be helpful:

"That's an interesting thought."

"I see what you mean."

"I'm glad you are taking an interest."

Sometimes parents unintentionally use "turn offs" when children talk. They ignore what the child says, change the subject, or pursue their own thoughts without listening at all. Some parents are apt to answer a child's conversation with:

"I haven't time to talk now."

"You talk too much."

"You're too young to know."

"You ask too many questions."

"Turn offs" deprive children of particularly good opportunities to comprehend language. "Turn offs" discourage children from asking questions. "Turn offs" also teach children that it is okay to not listen to others who speak to them. Parents are good role models for encouraging listening.

Speaking on the telephone is one more opportunity to encourage listening. Children benefit from taking part in telephone conversations.

Listening to the radio helps build listening comprehension, too.

Dad: Tim, shall we listen to "The Story Lady" program?

Tim: "Yeah, she tells good stories."

THE SILENT FAMILY

In some homes, the members of the family talk a lot to each other. In others, equally caring parents talk relatively little to their children. In some homes, children's curiosity is encouraged. In others, it is discouraged.

In the classroom, children from silent homes reflect their parent's personalities and the nature of their homes. Although the children may have superior mental ability, because they don't hear much conversation, they have less experience listening to oral language.

HOW READING TO YOUR CHILD INCREASES LISTENING COMPREHENSION

For smarter children with better grades, next to talking, nothing produces more magical results than reading a book. No activity

reaps more value for so little time, effort, and money. Children love to be read to. They enjoy sitting close to their parents, following the story with their fingers or their eyes. Children who are read to at home are more apt to enter school with enormous advantages, such as:

1. Their vocabulary is larger.

2. They comprehend the meaning of language better.

3. They are able to form mental images from words.

4. They are able to think more clearly.

5. They have more information about the world.

6. They are more creative and imaginative.

7. They concentrate better.

8. They express themselves better when they write or speak.

9. They learn new subjects more easily.

10. They learn that books are a source of lasting pleasure.

WHAT SHALL YOU READ?

When Daniel was six months old, his parents began reading to him. He didn't understand what they were saying, but he was attracted by pages with bright colors and shapes. As he grew older, his attention span increased and he understood more, especially when Mom and Dad used different voices for the different story characters. Some suggestions that work when parents read to their children are listed on the pages that follow.

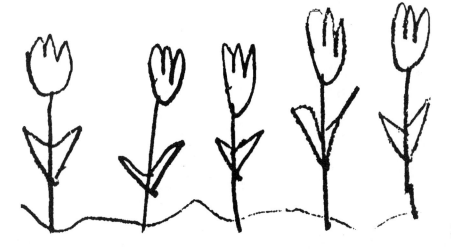

1. Begin with picturebooks of named objects, such as a ball, dog, car, toys, and so on. Before buying a picturebook, examine it to determine if the objects are easily recognizable for young children and if there are enough pages of objects to be worth the price of the book. Recently, we examined a book that contained only eight objects, two of which a child would rarely see. This was not a good book value.

2. Read Mother Goose rhymes. Choose books with attractive illustrations and many varieties of rhymes. Mother Goose is the most popular children's book of all time.

3. Along with Mother Goose rhymes, read old folk tales and fairy tales, such as "The Three Bears," "Chicken Little," and "Little Red Riding Hood."

4. For toddlers, preschoolers, and early elementary grade children, look for the Caldecott Medal winners. This is an annual award given since 1938 for the most distinguished children's picturebook published in the preceding year. Some Caldecott Medal books are available in paperback. The hardbacks can be found in most public libraries.

5. Choose books that stimulate the imagination.

6. Children also like stories and poems they do not entirely understand. They respond to the rhythm of words. Many children and adults love A. A. Milne's *When We Were Very Young* and *Winnie-the-Pooh*. In the library, there are collections of poems for children, ranging in subject matter from measles to mice.

7. Read the same stories over and over, a hundred times or more. Eventually your child learns every word in the story and comprehends every idea. This is what you are aiming for.

8. When your child is old enough, ask questions about the stories, but not so many as to interfere with the pleasure of listening.

9. Develop your child's love of books.

10. Plan special trips to the public library and let your child choose his or her own books.

11. Take books along in the car or while waiting for an appointment.

12. Take your child to the public library or community center to listen to storytime.

There are dozens of inexpensive books to buy in supermarkets and discount stores. For birthdays and holidays, beautifully illustrated hardbound books make treasured gifts. Otherwise, the public library offers a wide variety of books for your child to enjoy. There, you have the widest and best selection at the least cost.

HOW TO USE TELEVISION TO INCREASE LISTENING COMPREHENSION

Case History: Luke

Valentine's Day was fast approaching. The children in third grade were making animals designed from paper hearts. Luke raised his hand to speak.

Luke: I saw a movie last night on T.V. called "The St. Valentine's Day Massacre." It was great—but scary!

Teacher: What did you think of Al Capone? Did you like him?

Luke: Noooo! He was mean!

Luke learned about the St. Valentine's Day Massacre story from television. We aren't recommending that children watch such programs, but if television viewing is reinforced by discussions, opinions, and questions, it can be a valuable learning experience.

43

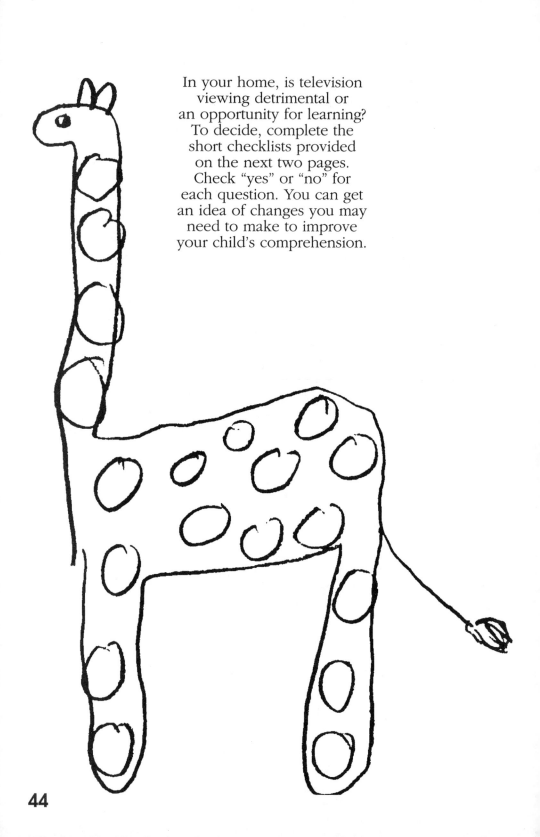

In your home, is television
viewing detrimental or
an opportunity for learning?
To decide, complete the
short checklists provided
on the next two pages.
Check "yes" or "no" for
each question. You can get
an idea of changes you may
need to make to improve
your child's comprehension.

Checklist 1

Following is a list of questions about typical home experiences. The questions will help you evaluate your child's ability to concentrate, understand, and respond appropriately. Some of the questions listed below may not be appropriate for all age levels. If this is the case, think of appropriate situations in which your child would need to listen to directions. Then ask yourself questions pertaining to those situations. Answer "yes" or "no" to each question.

		YES	NO
1.	Does your family watch and listen to television programs, one after the other, without discussion?	❏	❏
2.	While your family watches television, is the conversation limited to "Who wants a soda?" or "Shall I make some popcorn?"	❏	❏
3.	Does your child watch program after program by himself or herself in silence without interruption?	❏	❏
4.	When you ask your child what a program was about, does he or she respond with "I don't remember" or "I forgot"?	❏	❏
5.	Does your family watch and listen to commercials as silently as it listens to programs?	❏	❏

Several "yes" answers indicate that television is not being used as a learning tool in your home and you may want to make some changes in viewing habits.

4 to 5	needs improvement
2 to 3	average
0 to 1	good

Checklist 2

	YES	NO
1. While viewing television, does your family make comments about the program?	❏	❏
2. Do you use commercial times for discussing what you are viewing, including the commercials?	❏	❏
3. Does your child ask questions about what you are viewing?	❏	❏
4. When your child asks a question about a program you have just watched, do you sometimes say "That's a good question. Let's look it up."	❏	❏
5. Does your child talk about television programs?	❏	❏

Several "yes" answers indicates television is being used as a learning tool in your home.

4 to 5	good
2 to 3	average
0 to 1	needs improvement

IF USED PROPERLY, TELEVISION CAN INCREASE YOUR CHILD'S LISTENING COMPREHENSION

1. The language that children hear on television is reinforced by pictures. Visual clues help develop listening comprehension by showing what an idea or concept looks like.

2. Children hear and see information about science, geography, history, and current events that they may not be able to get from another source until they are much older.

3. Children can increase their vocabularies as they hear new words.

4. Television programs provide subject matter for conversations in which family members have an opportunity to listen to one another.

KINDS OF QUESTIONS TO ASK ABOUT TELEVISION

- Do you think a story like this happens in real life? How? Why not?

- Is the family on television like our family? Why?

- What didn't you like about the program?

- Do you believe what you saw on television?

- Why is this your favorite television program? Why is it better than other programs?

Television programs can be fuel for conversation and comprehension. One question asked will lead to another and before you realize it, you are having a good conversation with your child. You learn to listen to your child and your child learns to comprehend language from you. Helping your child improve his or her listening comprehension will lead to better grades in school.

Conversations with children improves their concentration and understanding. In the next chapter we will discuss the third component of listening—responding appropriately to what is said.

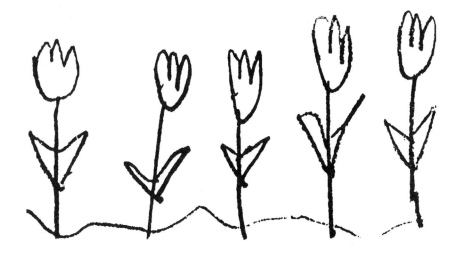

CHAPTER 5

RESPONSE: DOES YOUR CHILD REACT APPROPRIATELY?

If children pay attention and understand what they hear, what do they do? Some children do nothing. Some respond by storing the information for future use. Others use the information to make decisions about their own behavior or to ask questions. Some children respond with enjoyment, positive or negative attitudes, or a variety of emotions.

At home and at school, however, listening response is normally judged by how children behave. When mom asks Jimmy to take out the trash promptly and stop teasing his sister, does Jimmy do it? In school, after listening to his teacher explain a concept, does Jimmy know what she taught so that he can follow the directions for doing the assignment? On one occasion, Jimmy may do as he is supposed to and at another time he may not. In other words, Jimmy may respond with two types of behavior called *appropriate response* and *inappropriate response.*

APPROPRIATE RESPONSE

When given an assignment, the majority of children in an elementary classroom get down to work quickly. They pay attention to the teacher and try to understand what he or she said. They are eager to prove to themselves and to the teacher that they can do the assignment. They may not do it perfectly, but if the students need help, the teacher is there.

INAPPROPRIATE RESPONSE

In every classroom, a few children do not get down to work. They don't pay attention to the teacher or they may not understand him or her. They don't or won't do what they are supposed to do. Often parent-teacher conferences reveal that the behavior of these children is the same at home as it is in school.

An inappropriate response may include not paying attention to the directions, trying to listen and do something else, or disrupting another child's behavior or work habits. These responses are examples of not using good listening skills.

Occasionally, especially in the upper grades, a child may feel resentful or antagonized by a particular teacher and respond inappropriately. Some reasons for this type of behavior are found in the list on page 50.

WHY A CHILD MAY RESPOND
INAPPROPRIATELY AT SCHOOL

- May lack self-confidence

- Is tired after staying up late

- May not feel well

- May suffer from poor nutrition (may not have eaten breakfast)

- May have messy, disorganized habits

- May have emotional problems or be experiencing stress at home

- Feels defiant (does not want to be bossed around by adults)

- Cannot concentrate or does not understand what is being explained

- Is not in the habit of listening at home

- Does not do homework

- Is indifferent to school

- Feels too much pressure at home to get good grades

Children who respond in positive ways invariably do well in school. They learn and are self-confident and happy there. Teachers do not expect children to perform like robots, but they do know that a child who does not respond appropriately does not learn and is generally not a happy child.

APPROPRIATE RESPONSE AT HOME: FROM BIRTH TO AGE 5

"You gather more flies with honey than with vinegar."

When parents and teachers ask children to do something, life is much easier if the children simply do it. During our years in the classroom, we have learned how to win the cooperation of children, not every time and not every child, but most of the children and most of the time. The techniques we used, we believe, will work for parents as well as they did for us.

Years ago, a professor said to his class of young student teachers, "The best way to handle discipline is to avoid creating situations that demand it." Stated differently, it's the old adage: "An ounce of prevention is worth a pound of cure." The time to encourage appropriate listening responses is as early as you and your child can communicate with each other.

1. Begin with Praise

The quotation at the beginning of this section is worth repeating: "You gather more flies with honey than with vinegar." Praise makes children feel good about themselves. It puts them in a frame of mind to go along with the person who is doing the praising. It prompts an appropriate response. Harsh, critical words make children think badly about themselves. They feel antagonized, resentful, and resistant to doing what is asked of them. The result can be an inappropriate response.

Keep your eyes open for every possible opportunity, no matter how small, to praise your child, particularly when he or she listens and follows directions.

Even a smile and a hug is sweet praise to a child's ears.

"What a good baby... a good, good baby!"

"What a good job you did dressing yourself, Jamal!"

"You did a nice job, Jessica."

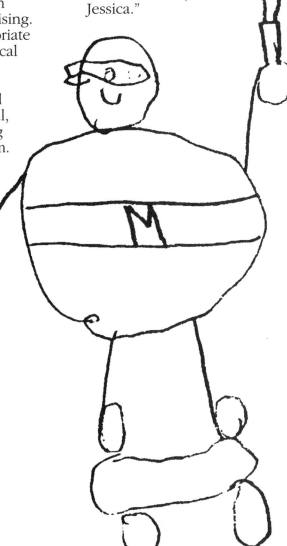

"Marvelous! You did exactly what mommy asked you to do."

"You finished on time. Great!"

"You were careful and did not hurry. Excellent."

"You're a helpful person, Ben. Thank you."

"Splendid! Thank you, Anna. I didn't realize you could follow directions so well."

"That's wonderful, Josh. You did a fine job!"

2. Prepare Your Child Beforehand for the Response You Want

Father: (Making sure that four-year-old Shawn is looking at him, he speaks quietly and without threats.) Shawn, we're going to McDonald's as I promised. Do you remember how to act in a restaurant?

Shawn: I have to sit still.

Father: Good. What else?

Shawn: I'm not going to make a mess.

Father: Fine! And we'll all talk quietly. O.K.?

Shawn: O.K.

Father: You have a good memory, Shawn. It's fun to eat out, isn't it?

Before going to a friend's or relative's home, or to a public place where you would like your child to be well-mannered, ask your child to concentrate on what you are about to say. Speak quietly, but firmly, and look your child straight in the eye. Do not make threatening statements. Rather, let your tone of voice impart this message:

"I know you want to behave well at Aunt Ellie's. She will be surprised to see what a good listener you are.

Would you like to take a book and a toy with you?"

53

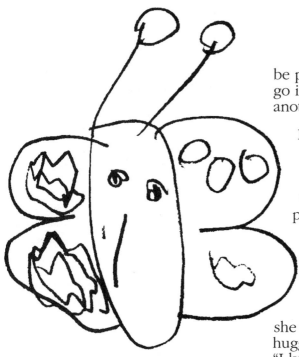

be patient while parents go into one store after another.

In the above situation, mother has her problem, but Theo has his, too. He is too tired to respond positively. Mother is expecting too much of Theo and she makes matters worse by yelling at him. If mother must finish the shopping, she will ease matters by hugging Theo and saying "I know you're tired. I have just one more thing to buy. Then we will go home and have dinner." This action tells Theo that his mother is aware of how he feels and that she will try to meet his needs as soon as possible.

3. Make Reasonable Requests

Mother: Theo, please stand up on your own two feet and walk. I have all these packages to carry.

Theo: (A tired three-year-old, whines and drags his feet.)

Mother: Now stop that!

Embarrassing scenes like this occur daily in supermarkets and shopping malls. Parents, pressed for time, must take little children with them while they shop. Still, it is unreasonable to expect children to

4. Accustom Your Child to Respond to Your Natural Tone of Voice

Mother: John, stop pouring the milk into your soup. If you don't want more soup, then just leave it.

John: (Makes a gesture to continue.)

Mother: (Silently removes John's soup bowl from his place. If John's mealtime is over, she removes him from the table, too.)

In the above example, Mother spoke in a natural tone of voice. She did not repeat her request two or three times. She acted in such a manner that John received this message: I must follow directions the first time I am told.

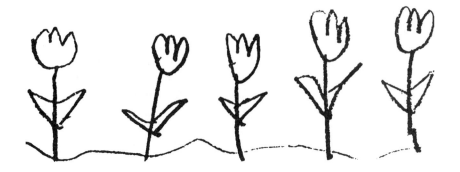

HOW WELL DOES MY CHILD RESPOND?

Answer the following questions "yes" or "no."

Does my child: YES   NO

1. Have difficulty following one, two, or three-step directions?   ❏   ❏

2. Deliberately ignore me when he or she is called by name?   ❏   ❏

3. Have to be called several times before answering?   ❏   ❏

4. Do the opposite of what I say?   ❏   ❏

5. Ignore what I say?   ❏   ❏

6. Become confused about what to do?   ❏   ❏

7. Need lots of reminders?   ❏   ❏

8. Argue with me about what I said?   ❏   ❏

Several "yes" answers may show your child has a problem with responding appropriately.

6 to 8	needs improvement
3 to 5	average
0 to 2	good

CHAPTER 6

TEACHING YOUR CHILD APPROPRIATE LISTENING RESPONSES: AGES 5 TO 10

Even if your child is ten years old and hasn't learned to listen well, it is not too late to teach him or her. How can you tell if your child has a listening problem?

Here are some clues.

Look for a listening problem if:

1. You talk to your child and a quizzical look appears on his or her face.

2. You talk to your child and he or she remains silent or becomes sullen.

3. You give your child a direction and he or she does the opposite or only part of what you asked.

4. You tell your child to do something and he or she pays no attention.

Poor behavior often results from poor listening habits. Fortunately, you can reteach your child to listen.

GUIDELINES FOR TEACHING YOUR CHILD TO LISTEN: AGES 5 TO 10

Objective 1. To Teach Your Child to Listen and Follow Directions Accurately

Does this happen in your home?

You give your child these directions: "Ernie, would you go down to the basement to get a can of spaghetti sauce? On the left of the stairs you'll find the cupboards where I keep the canned goods.

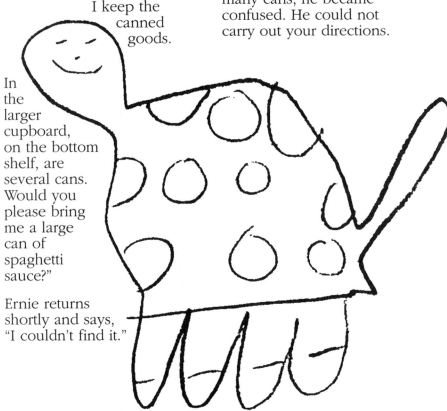

In the larger cupboard, on the bottom shelf, are several cans. Would you please bring me a large can of spaghetti sauce?"

Ernie returns shortly and says, "I couldn't find it."

You repeat the instructions and Ernie returns a second time, this time with a large can of vegetable soup.

What Happened?

Ernie did not concentrate completely on your directions. He heard two key ideas: large can and cupboard. He did not pay attention to the other words you used. Before you finished with the directions, he was headed for the basement. There, confronted by two cupboards, numerous shelves, and many cans, he became confused. He could not carry out your directions.

What Should You Do?

1. Get your child's attention and maintain eye contact.

2. Give your directions carefully and clearly.

3. Ask your child to repeat the directions.

When giving directions, stop whatever you are doing, concentrate on your child, and make certain he or she is ready to concentrate completely on you. Look your child in the eye and say, "I'm going to give you a set of directions. Are you ready to listen?" Give the directions slowly, emphasizing the detail words, such as "two cupboards," "bottom shelf," "large can," and "spaghetti sauce." Then say, "Now, tell me what you're going to look for."

Insist that your child pay attention until you are finished giving all the directions. If he or she has a tendency to rush off before you are done, have him or her sit on a chair while you talk. If you sit near your child while giving directions, that is even better.

ACHIEVING YOUR GOAL

The ability to listen and follow spoken directions is important to success in school. Remember: Be persistent! Be patient! Be quick to praise!

Objective 2. Teach Your Child to Listen and Follow Simple Requests Promptly

Does this happen in your home?

Jesse is watching television. You call to her three times to change her clothes because she has a dental appointment. She continues to watch television and you scold her for not listening.

What Happened?

Either the television program was so interesting that Jesse decided to ignore what you said, or, she didn't see the importance of changing her clothes merely to go to the dentist.

What Should You Do?

1. Don't interrupt something important to your child unless it is really necessary. The above example was necessary, but constant interruption of your child's activities often encourages a child to tune out all requests over time—whether necessary or not.

2. Get your child's attention and maintain eye contact.

3. Give your directions or requests clearly.

4. Stay with your child long enough to see him or her begin following your request. (In the beginning, you may need to stay the entire time it takes your child to complete the request.)

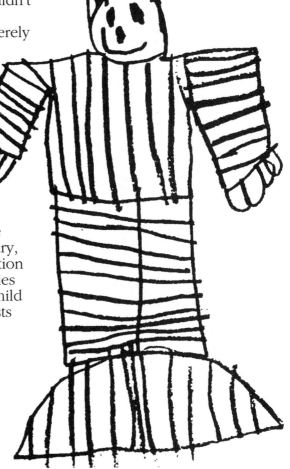

5. Do not call orders out to your child from another room. Go into the room where he or she is.

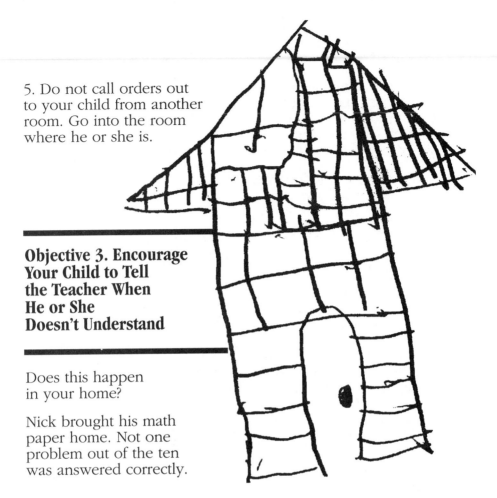

Objective 3. Encourage Your Child to Tell the Teacher When He or She Doesn't Understand

Does this happen in your home?

Nick brought his math paper home. Not one problem out of the ten was answered correctly.

What Is Happening?

Either Nick did not concentrate on the assignment, or he did not understand when Mr. MacHale explained what to do. When it came time to do the assignment, Nick was too embarrassed to tell Mr. MacHale that he didn't understand how to do the problems. Nick was afraid the other children would think he was dumb.

What Should You Do?

1. Let your child know you will be supportive, no matter what the problem.

2. Explain that it's "smart" to let the teacher know when you don't understand something.

3. Offer help and reinforce the notion that if your child listens and pays attention, he or she will learn more in school.

61

This is not a time to scold or punish Nick. Encourage him to go up to the teacher and say "I don't understand." For example:

Dad: Not a very good paper, is it Nick? I'll bet you feel bad about it.

Nick: (Remains silent.)

Dad: Can you tell me what the problem was?

Nick: I didn't know what he was talking about.

Dad: It's good that you are saying that. That helps me understand why you missed the problems. Did you pay attention while Mr. MacHale was explaining?

Nick: Some.

Dad: Well that's a good place to begin. There's no way anyone in your class is going to learn to do the problems unless they pay close attention. Did you tell Mr. MacHale you didn't understand?

Nick: No.

Dad: Now let me help you with the problems. If you pay attention, you'll get it. You're a smart boy, Nick. Anything I say that you don't understand, just ask me. Okay?

Nick had a hard time doing his math because he was not using good listening skills. He wasn't paying attention when the teacher explained how to do the problems, therefore he didn't understand what to do when the assignment was given. In the end, Nick's response was inappropriate because he tried to complete the math problems without understanding the concepts. An appropriate response to this situation would have been for Nick to tell his teacher that he needed extra help.

Parents can be good role models by admitting to their children when they do not understand something. For example:

"I can't figure out what's wrong with the washer. I guess we'll have to call a service person after all."

"I don't understand these directions. I'm going to call Helen for help."

Some children never say a word in the classroom because they are afraid of being wrong. Children should know that it's okay to make mistakes. In truth, we learn more from our mistakes than from our successes. Children will get this message if they see their parents freely admitting their mistakes and praising their children for doing the same. These behavior patterns, learned at home, transfer to the classroom and help children earn better grades.

Objective 4. Teach Your Child to Think About What the Teacher Is Saying

Does this happen in your home?

Jeff's favorite activity is watching television. He

often watches hours of television without ever talking to anyone.

What Is Happening?

Let's suppose that Ms. Riley is talking to the children in class about reading maps. She expects them to listen and get the main idea of what she is saying, to remember a few details, and have some thoughts of their own. For Jeff, who is in the habit of watching television for endless hours, listening has become a passive act. He does not have the habit of questioning nor thinking about what he is viewing. While Ms. Riley is explaining a new lesson to the class, Jeff listens to her in the same way he listens to television.

What Should You Do?

1. Watch television with your child.

2. Ask questions about television programs beginning with the five W's: "who," "what," "where," "when," and "why."

As soon as your child can follow a television program and understand what is going on, begin watching television with him or her and talk about the programs—even the commercials.
When Mom and Dad watch television with Jeff, or when eating, driving, or getting ready for bed, they ask him questions that begin with the five W's: "who?" "what?" "when?" "where?" and "why?" For example:

Who is the hero? Did you like him or her?

Where did the story take place?

When (past or present) did the story take place?

What was the bad guy trying to do? Why did he act that way?

What would have made the story better?

When Jeff becomes accustomed to thinking as he is listening and watching, every television program becomes a teacher from whom he learns. He can then listen to his teacher in the same thoughtful way.

Mom and Dad can encourage Jeff to listen to one or two stories in the news every day and ask questions about them. It's surprising how many children in first grade pick up bits and pieces of the daily news from television at home.

HOW PLAYING GAMES TEACHES CHILDREN TO LISTEN

Many of the suggestions we have made throughout this book for teaching children to listen can be reinforced by playing games. Games demand concentration, understanding, and responding appropriately. Playing the simplest of card games or board games, such as "Candyland" or "Shoots and Ladders," requires that children pay attention to directions, understand what they have to do, and then play the game according to the rules.

In the following chapter, we describe thirteen games that require no equipment and can be played almost anywhere.

CHAPTER 7

GAMES MAKE LISTENING FUN!

Teaching your child to listen takes patience and persistence. Listening games are not a substitute for your daily effort, but they will reinforce listening skills in a way that is lots of fun. The games described here are simple to play and encourage children to listen.

When playing a listening game, try to keep it natural. Your child will resist your efforts if he or she feels the game is supposed to "teach" something. That takes the fun away. When playing a game, avoid saying to your child, "You're wrong." Accept all answers by saying, "That's interesting," or, "Let's see if there's another possible answer."

Rewards may be helpful to learning. With young children, a smile, a hug, and words of praise are often sufficient. With school-age children, you might devise a system for accumulating points. For a certain number of points, give your child a reward. Depending on the child's age and the number of

points accumulated, the reward can be a sticker, a colored pencil or pen, or a favorite food for dinner. It is important to encourage children to work hard in order to be successful in school, rather than just accumulate prize points.

We Listen Better When We're Not Under Stress! Games Are for Fun!

GAMES FOR PRESCHOOLERS

❤ MISSING WORDS ❤

How to Play

Tell or read to your child a familiar story. As you read, omit words at critical places. Encourage your child to fill in the missing words. This game seems simple, but children really enjoy it.

Example

Once upon a time there were three bears. There was a mama bear, a papa bear, and a wee little baby _____.

Variation

When the game becomes too easy, try leaving out more difficult words. Then try more difficult stories.

❤ SOUND EFFECTS ❤

How to Play

Assign different sound effects to one or more children. Sounds can be of any type, such as a cow, cat, dog, crying, laughing, clocks, wind, airplane, and whistle. Then make up a story, however silly, about these animals and objects. Excellent Halloween stories can be made up with your child or children making sounds for goblins and ghosts at the appropriate places in the story.

Example

Once there was a cat. (Child assigned cat sound, meows.) The cat (cat sound effect) met a dog (dog sound effect). The cat (cat sound effect) and the dog (dog sound effect) met a cow (cow sound effect). The animals (all three sounds) went for a walk. Everybody began laughing (all three sounds) because they sounded so funny (and so on).

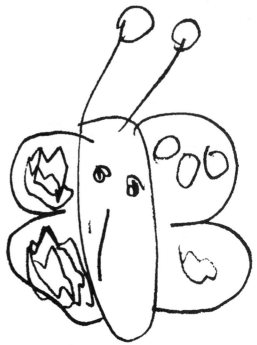

❤ WHAT SOUNDS DO ❤ YOU HEAR?

How to Play

This game can be played while shopping in the supermarket, at the mall, while walking, or in your own home. Ask your child to name a sound he or she hears. Your child's eyes can be opened, covered, or closed, depending on the place. After naming the sound, ask your child to tell what could be happening that would cause the sound to be made. This simple game gives your child experience in concentrating in order to identify the sound. The discussion about the sound develops comprehension.

Examples of Sounds

a horn
buzz
a peep
a funny voice
cash register
crying
laughing
auto starting
scratching
doorbell
hammer tapping
bus starting
helicopter
electric clock
door closing
door opening
wind
car squeak
wheels squealing
truck passing

❤ NAME MY STORY ❤

How to Play

While working about the house, out walking, driving in a car, or wherever you are, make up a short story about what you are doing. Then ask your child to give the story a name. This type of game teaches children to listen for the main idea. It teaches both concentration and comprehension. Discuss why one title might be better than another.

1. After breakfast, the family decided to go to the shopping center. First, we got into our car. We drove down Locust Street and turned onto Route 19. We kept driving until we reached Southland Mall.

   What would you say is a good title for this story?

2. This morning I have a lot of work to do. After I check the mail, I am going to write some letters. But, before I start the letters, I am going to make some phone calls.

   What title would you give this story?

Variation

Let members of the family take turns making up the stories. The subjects can be expanded to include imaginary, humorous, or ridiculous stories.

❤ WORD SUBS ❤

How to Play

Say two or three sentences that are exactly alike, except for one word. Ask your child to identify the changes in the sentences. Try other substitutions as well. This game prompts children to listen carefully. They learn that every word in a sentence is important. The substitution of a single word, or the omission of a word, changes the meaning of the sentence. This is a particularly good game to play when driving in a car.

Examples

I folded your *shirt* and put it into your drawer.

I folded your *undershirt* and put it into your drawer.

I *ironed* your shirt and put it into your drawer.

Did you see that *black and white* cow with its calf in the field?

Did you see that *black* cow with its calf in the field?

Did you see that black and white cow with its calf in the *barn*?

Variation

Use the same sentence, but in each sentence, emphasize a different word by the tone of your voice. See if your child can hear the difference. The emphasized word is italicized.

I saw a *brown* cow by that red barn.

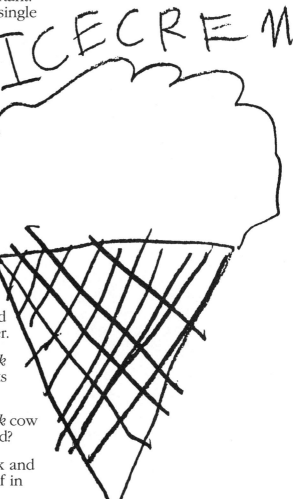

71

I saw a brown cow by that red barn.

I saw a brown cow by *that* red barn.

I saw a brown cow by that *red* barn.

❤ TELEPHONE ❤ NUMBER

How to Play

Say a series of individual numbers. See how many numbers your child can repeat.

Gradually increase the number of digits. Say the digits individually. Do not say: two-thousand-six hundred-thirty-six.

Interest in this game will increase if a "point" is given each time an additional digit is remembered beyond the original number of digits. Your child will be pleased to see how many points he or she can earn.

Example

2-6-3-6. Can your child repeat the numbers in the exact order? 2-6-3-6-9? 2-6-3-6-9-4?

❤ THROW ONE BACK ❤

How to Play

Name three objects or more (depending upon the child's age) of a similar category, except for one. In other words, one object should not fit the category. The child "throws back" the object that doesn't fit. This game encourages children to think as well as listen. Through selecting less commonly used words, it can also expand a child's vocabulary. The child, too, can originate groups of words for others to "throw back."

Example

orange, banana, *hamburger*, apple

eraser, pencil, pen,
felt tip marker

happy, smiling,
cheerful, *sad*

The italicized words are
the words that would be
"thrown back."

Variation

A "thrown back" word can
become the category for a
new group of words.

Almost all the games
described here can be
modified to challenge older
children.

GAMES FOR CHILDREN AGES 5 TO 10

❤ DIRECTIONS ❤

How to Play

Give a series of directions
only once. Ask your child
to follow them. Give
praise or a small token
reward if the directions
are followed correctly.
Make a game of following
directions. Here are some
examples of directions
you might ask your child
to follow.

Say to your child:

(In the kitchen) Place a box of cornflakes in the center of the table. Place a pitcher of milk and a bowl of sugar by the cornflakes. Set four bowls on the table, four spoons, and four napkins.

(In the car) Look out the right window and name one thing you see. Look out the left window and name one thing you see. Look on the floor of the car and name two things that you see.

(At bedtime) Walk backwards to your closet. Get your pajamas and put them on. Get into bed by climbing in from the foot of the bed. Lie down on your stomach and put the pillow over your head.

(To get to the car after shopping) Take five skips, three hops, eight baby steps, and four giant steps.

❤ WHO? WHAT? WHEN? ❤ WHERE? WHY?

How to Play

Say to your child:

"I am going to read (or tell) you a story. When I am done, see if you can answer these questions: Who? What? When? Where? Why?" Give a reward if all the questions are answered. The questions "who," "what," "when," "why," and "where," are important when listening and when reading. With practice, children automatically listen for them, thereby improving listening comprehension.

Sample Story

Toni and her companion, Aaron, were hiking in the Sandia Mountains on Saturday when they got lost late that after-noon. The two hikers had to spend the night in below-freezing temperatures. Rescuers

were alerted and set out to find the two hikers early Sunday morning. The hikers were found, cold but unharmed, by the rescuers about noon on Sunday.

❤ I'M GOING ON A TRIP ❤

How to Play

One person begins by saying, "I am going on a trip and I am going to take a book with me." The next person repeats what has been said and adds one more object. The person who remembers the most objects in the order mentioned is the winner. This game develops concentration and memory. Vary the game by taking a trip to another state or country, an amusement park, a picnic, or even another planet.

Example

First person: I am going on a trip and I am going to take a book with me.

Second person: I am going on a trip and I am going to take a book and a pillow with me.

Third person: I am going on a trip and I am going to take a book, a pillow, and a map with me.

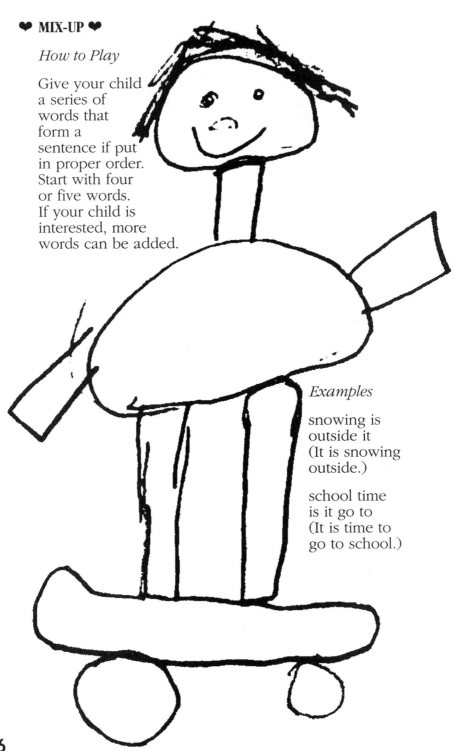

❤ MIX-UP ❤

How to Play

Give your child a series of words that form a sentence if put in proper order. Start with four or five words. If your child is interested, more words can be added.

Examples

snowing is outside it
(It is snowing outside.)

school time is it go to
(It is time to go to school.)

❤ LITTLE WORDS MEAN A LOT ❤

How to Play

Read or tell a story to your child. Ask him or her to make a little mark with a pencil on a paper every time he or she hears a particular character's name. Give a token reward if he or she hears the selected word every time it appears in the story.

Variation

Instead of a character's name, ask your child to listen for a kind of word, such as food words, weather words, or words describing people.

❤ ARRANGE THE OBJECTS ❤

How to Play

Place 6 to 8 objects on a table. Then name the objects in a particular order. Ask your child to pick the objects up in the order named.

Example

Place a pencil, rubberband, spoon, button, raisin, toy car, and so on on the table. Then ask your child to pick the objects up in the order you name them.
For example: car, button,

spoon, pencil, raisin, rubberband. If your child picks the objects up in the correct order, he or she gets to eat a raisin.

Variation

For older children, 10 or 12 objects can be used. For fun, let your child name the objects and see if you can pick them up in the named order.

Children can learn to be keen listeners through riddles, poems, music, sound effects, radio, cassettes, and television. As your child is preparing to listen, ask him or her a question that will direct his or her listening and cause him or her to listen more intently.

For example:

Who has the highest voice?

Who has the lowest voice?

Who was unhappy?

Who spoke the most?

Who was the meanest?

How old are the people?

Is the story real or make-believe?

Let your child know that listening is important by what you say and what you do. Remember the three components of listening: concentration, understanding, and response. With a little effort, listening can become a habit that will help your child earn better grades and eventually live a life that is easier and fuller.

FUN BOOKS TO READ WITH YOUR CHILD

Caps for Sale by Esphyr Slobodkina

Charlotte's Web by E. B. White

Chickens Aren't the Only Ones by Ruth Heller

Corduroy by Don Freeman

Curious George by H. A. Rey

Drummer Hoff by Ed Emberley

Goodnight Moon by Margaret Wise Brown

Henry and Ribsy by Beverly Cleary

James and the Giant Peach by Roald Dahl

Lon Po Po: A Red-Riding Hood Story from China translated by Ed Young and edited by Patricia Gauch

Mother Goose Nursery Rhymes by Supper Chubby Books

Polar Express by Chris Van Allsburg

A Snowy Day by Ezra Jack Keats

Superfudge by Judy Blume

Tuck Everlasting by Natalie Babbitt

When We Were Very Young by A. A. Milne

Where the Sidewalk Ends by Shel Silverstein

Where the Wild Things Are by Maurice Sendak

Why Mosquitoes Buzz in People's Ears by Verna Aardema

Wilfrid Gordon McDonald Partridge by Mem Fox

Winnie-the-Pooh by A. A. Milne